**1**

# What color is this pumpkin?

D1801267

A ● yellow

B ● orange

C ● red

**2**

# What color is this shoe?

A ● red

B ● purple

C ● green

**3**

# What color is this frog?

A ⬤ yellow

B ⬤ blue

C ⬤ green

**4**

# What color is this fire truck?

A ⬤ pink

B ⬤ red

C ⬤ purple

**5** What color are these jeans?

A ● yellow

B ● green

C ● blue

**6** What color is the sun?

A ● yellow

B ● brown

C ● blue

## 7

**What color is this tire?**

A ⬤ brown

B ⬤ black

C ⬤ white

## 8

**What color is this bear?**

A ⬤ green

B ⬤ blue

C ⬤ brown

**9**

# What color is this bubble?

A ⬤ purple

B ⬤ pink

C ⬤ red

**10**

# What color is this milk?

A ⬤ white

B ⬤ yellow

C ⬤ orange

## 11

**What color is this elephant?**

A ⬤ white

B ⬤ black

C ⬤ gray

## 12

**What color is this crayon?**

A ⬤ red

B ⬤ blue

C ⬤ yellow

# What color is this crayon?

A ⬤ yellow

B ⬤ orange

C ⬤ green

# What color is this crayon?

A ⬤ blue

B ⬤ green

C ⬤ yellow

**15** What color is this crayon?

A ● green

B ● blue

C ● pink

**16** What color is this crayon?

A ● pink

B ● blue

C ● red

## 17

**What color is this crayon?**

A ⬤ black

B ⬤ purple

C ⬤ pink

## 18

**What color is this crayon?**

A ⬤ purple

B ⬤ pink

C ⬤ gray

## 19

**What color is this crayon?**

A ● brown

B ● blue

C ● black

## 20

**What color is this crayon?**

A ● black

B ● brown

C ● blue

## 21

**What color is this crayon?**

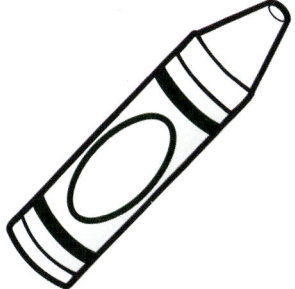

A ⬤ white

B ⬤ purple

C ⬤ green

## 22

**What color is this crayon?**

A ⬤ green

B ⬤ gray

C ⬤ red

## 23 Can you find green?

A

C

B

D

## 24 Can you find red?

A

C

B

D

## Can you find white?

A ⬬

C ⬬

B ⬬

D ⬬

## Can you find blue?

A ⬬

C ⬬

B ⬬

D ⬬

## 27 Can you find **purple**?

A ⬤ 　　C ⬤

B ⬤ 　　D ⬤

## 28 Can you find **yellow**?

A ⬤ 　　C ⬤

B ⬤ 　　D ⬤

**29** Can you find orange?

A ⬤

C ⬤

B ⬤

D ⬤

**30** Can you find gray?

A ⬤

C ⬤

B ⬤

D ⬤

## 31

### Can you find black?

A

B

C

D

## 32

### Can you find pink?

A

B

C

D

## 33

Can you find brown?

A ⬤

C ⬤

B ⬤

D ⬤

## 34

This car is _____.

A ⬤ red

B ⬤ yellow

C ⬤ blue

**35**

This carrot is _____.

A ● orange

B ● purple

C ● blue

**36**

This chair is _____.

A ● orange

B ● blue

C ● brown

**37** This chick is _____.

A ⬤ red

B ⬤ yellow

C ⬤ white

**38** This can is _____.

A ⬤ yellow

B ⬤ purple

C ⬤ green

**39**

This cup is _____.

A ⬤ purple

B ⬤ pink

C ⬤ red

**40**

This lettuce is _____.

A ⬤ red

B ⬤ yellow

C ⬤ green

**41** This pig is _____.

A ⬤ white

B ⬤ orange

C ⬤ pink

**42** This bag is _____.

A ⬤ white

B ⬤ brown

C ⬤ pink

**43** This swan is _____.

A ⬤ pink

B ⬤ brown

C ⬤ white

**44** These glasses are _____.

A ⬤ brown

B ⬤ black

C ⬤ gray

**45** Find a circle.

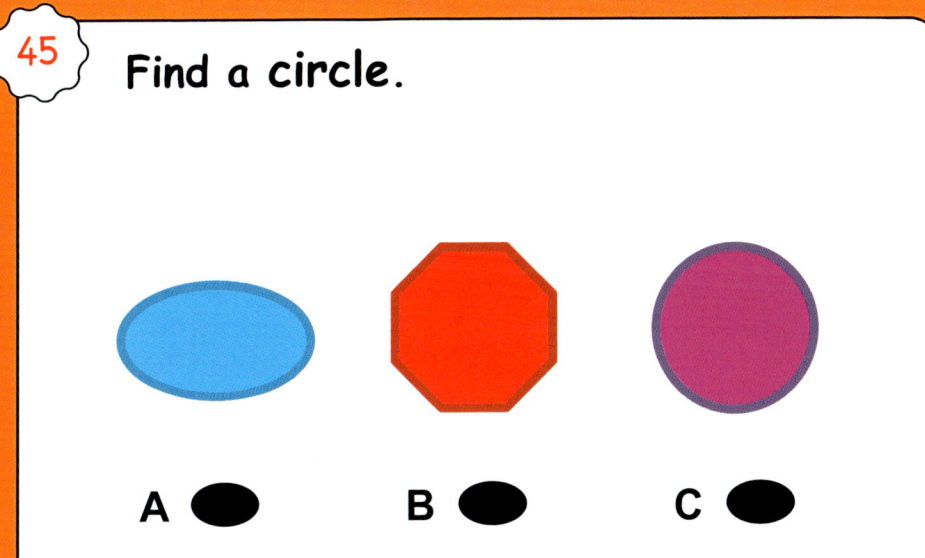

A ●     B ●     C ●

**46** Find a square.

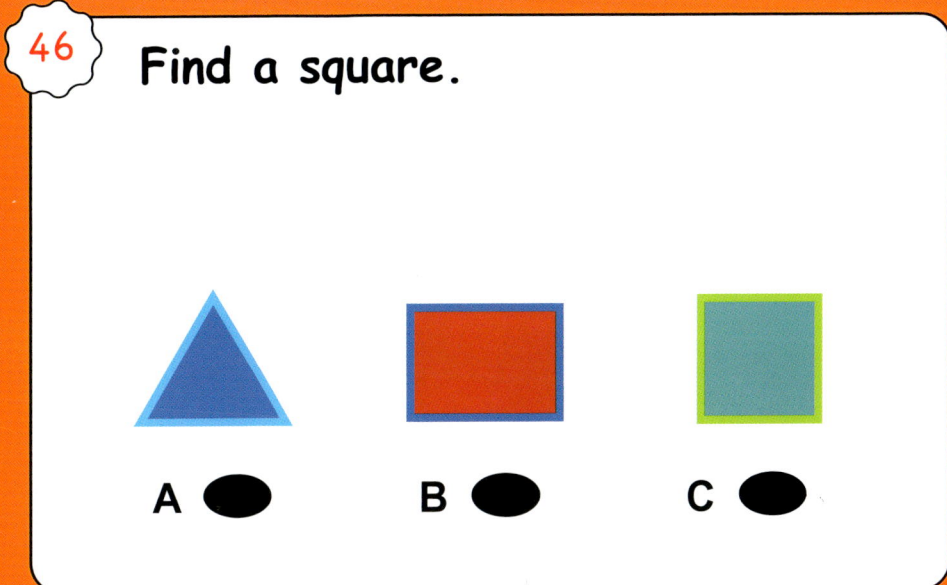

A ●     B ●     C ●

**47** Find an oval.

A ⬮    B ⬮    C ⬮

**48** Find a rectangle.

A ⬮    B ⬮    C ⬮

**49** Find a triangle.

A ⬤    B ⬤    C ⬤

**50** Find a hexagon.

A ⬤    B ⬤    C ⬤

## 51

Find a rhombus.

A    B   C

## 52

Find a pentagon.

A   B   C

## Find an octagon.

A      B ⬤     C ⬤

---

## Find a cube.

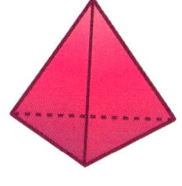  

A      B ⬤     C ⬤

## 55 Find a cone.

A ⬤    B ⬤    C ⬤

## 56 Find a sphere.

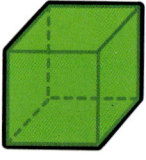  

A ⬤    B ⬤    C ⬤

**57** Find a cylinder.

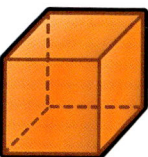  

A ⬤     B ⬤     C ⬤

**58** This shape is a _____.

A ⬤ triangle

B ⬤ cone

C ⬤ circle

**59**

These shapes are _____.

A ⬤ cubes

B ⬤ cones

C ⬤ spheres

**60**

This shape is a _____.

A ⬤ rectangle

B ⬤ sphere

C ⬤ square

**61** This shape is a _____.

A ⬤ sphere

B ⬤ prism

C ⬤ cone

**62** This shape is a _____.

A ⬤ square

B ⬤ rectangle

C ⬤ hexagon

**63**

This shape is a _____.

A ⬤ circle

B ⬤ square

C ⬤ oval

**64**

This shape is a _____.

A ⬤ rhombus

B ⬤ square

C ⬤ triangle

## 65

This shape is an _____.

A ⬤ square

B ⬤ octagon

C ⬤ triangle

## 66

This hat is a _____.

A ⬤ cylinder

B ⬤ prism

C ⬤ cone

**67**

This ball is a _____.

A ⬭ cylinder

B ⬭ sphere

C ⬭ cone

---

**68**

# Which shape is not a triangle?

A ⬭        B ⬭        C ⬭

**69** Which shape is not a square?

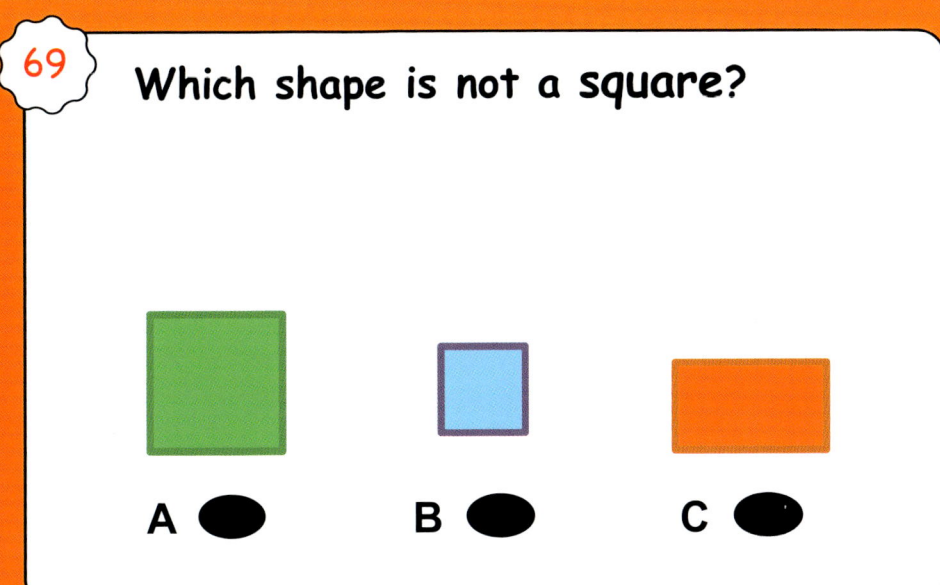

A ⬤     B ⬤     C ⬤

**70** Which shape is not a rectangle?

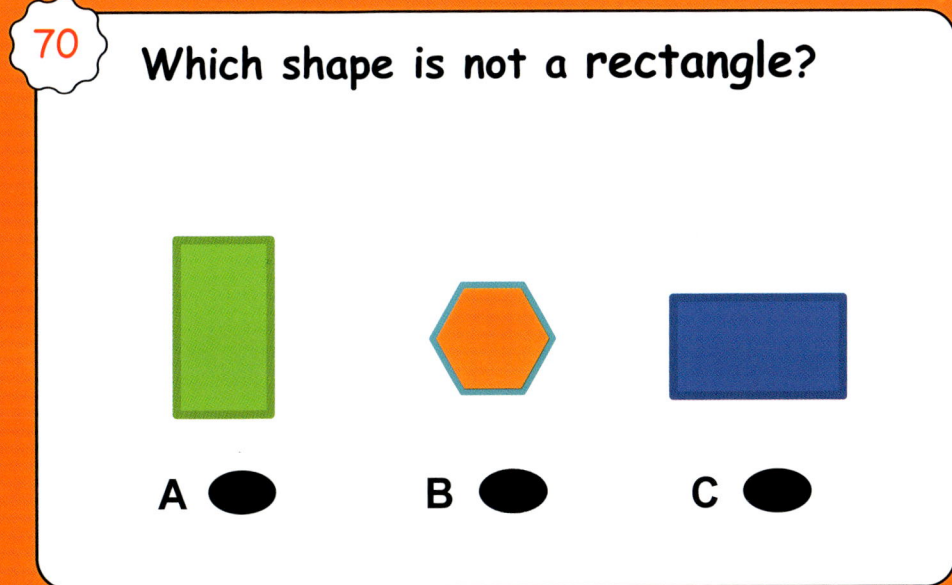

A ⬤     B ⬤     C ⬤

# Which shape is not a circle?

A     B    C

---

# Which shape is not an oval?

A    B    C

# Which shape is not a cone?

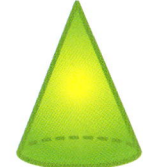

A ⬤    B ⬤    C ⬤

# Which shape is not a sphere?

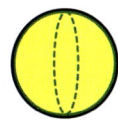

A ⬤    B ⬤    C ⬤

# Which shape is not a cube?

  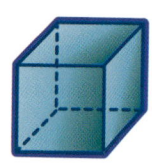  

A ⬤          B ⬤          C ⬤

# Which shape is not an octagon?

A ⬤          B ⬤          C ⬤

**Which shape is not a hexagon?**

A ⬤     B ⬤     C ⬤

**Which shape is not a pentagon?**

A ⬤     B ⬤     C ⬤

# How many sides does a rhombus have?

A ⬤ 5

B ⬤ 3

C ⬤ 4

# How many sides does a square have?

A ⬤ 4

B ⬤ 6

C ⬤ 5